EVE AND HER SISTERS

Women of the Old Testament

PAINTINGS BY
MALCAH ZELDIS
WORDS BY **YONA ZELDIS McDONOUGH**

GREENWILLOW BOOKS, NEW YORK

This book is lovingly dedicated to Tania Brightman,
mother and grandmother.
—M. Z. and Y. Z. M.

ALL BIBLICAL QUOTES ARE TAKEN FROM
THE AUTHORIZED KING JAMES VERSION OF THE HOLY BIBLE.

THE FULL-COLOR ARTWORK WAS PREPARED WITH GOUACHE PAINTS ON PAPER.
THE TEXT TYPE IS ITC BEMBO.
ILLUSTRATIONS COPYRIGHT © 1994 BY MALCAH ZELDIS
TEXT COPYRIGHT © 1994 BY YONA ZELDIS McDONOUGH
ALL RIGHTS RESERVED. NO PART OF THIS BOOK MAY BE REPRODUCED OR UTILIZED IN ANY FORM
OR BY ANY MEANS, ELECTRONIC OR MECHANICAL, INCLUDING PHOTOCOPYING, RECORDING,
OR BY ANY INFORMATION STORAGE AND RETRIEVAL SYSTEM,
WITHOUT PERMISSION IN WRITING FROM THE PUBLISHER,
GREENWILLOW BOOKS, A DIVISION OF WILLIAM MORROW & COMPANY, INC.,
1350 AVENUE OF THE AMERICAS, NEW YORK, NY 10019.
PRINTED IN SINGAPORE BY TIEN WAH PRESS
FIRST EDITION 10 9 8 7 6 5 4 3 2 1

LIBRARY OF CONGRESS CATALOGING-IN-PUBLICATION DATA
McDONOUGH, YONA ZELDIS.
EVE AND HER SISTERS: WOMEN OF THE OLD TESTAMENT /
BY YONA ZELDIS McDONOUGH ;
PICTURES BY MALCAH ZELDIS.
P.   CM.
SUMMARY: PRESENTS BRIEF STORIES OF FOURTEEN WOMEN
WHO ARE MENTIONED IN THE OLD TESTAMENT, INCLUDING
EVE, RUTH, HAGAR, AND DEBORAH.
ISBN 0-688-12512-3 (TRADE).   ISBN 0-688-12513-1 (LIB. BDG.)
1. WOMEN IN THE BIBLE—JUVENILE LITERATURE.
[1. WOMEN IN THE BIBLE.   2. BIBLE STORIES—O.T.]
I. ZELDIS, MALCAH, ILL.   II. TITLE   BS575.M38   1994
221.9'22'082—DC20   93-9378   CIP   AC

CONTENTS

...she took of the fruit...
and did eat....
GENESIS 3:6

EVE TASTES THE FRUIT

Eve and Adam were the very first woman and man on Earth. God had created them and the beautiful Garden of Eden in which they lived as husband and wife. Eve knew that she was not supposed to eat the fruit of a certain tree that grew in the middle of the garden, for God had forbidden it. There were many other trees, so she spent her days eating their ripe fruit, smelling their fragrant flowers, and stroking the gentle animals that wandered beneath their boughs.

But one day she met a serpent that beguiled her into tasting the fruit of the forbidden tree. The fruit was delicious, and Eve offered it to Adam, who ate of it, too. Suddenly God appeared, angry at their disobedience. As punishment Eve and Adam were forced to leave the Garden of Eden, never again to return.

*...God hath made me to laugh,
so that all that hear
will laugh with me.*
GENESIS 21:6

SARAH'S JOY

Sarah was overjoyed! After years of waiting she was finally expecting a child. She and Abraham, her husband, had almost stopped hoping for one. So when three mysterious strangers appeared at their tent promising a miracle, Sarah had not believed them. "How can an old woman like me have a baby?" she had asked. But the voice of God had answered, "Nothing is too difficult for me."

And sure enough, a year later Sarah gave birth to a son. To show her happiness, she called him Isaac, which means "He laughs."

*And she sat over against him,
and lift up her voice, and wept.*
GENESIS 21:16

HAGAR
IN THE
WILDERNESS

Hagar the Egyptian was Sarah's maid. Hagar had borne a son to Abraham. He was called Ishmael. But when Sarah's son Isaac was born, Sarah made Abraham send Hagar away. Hagar and Ishmael wandered through the hot desert. When their food and water were gone, Ishmael lay down under a bush. Hagar began to weep. "Let me not see the death of my child," she said. But then she heard an angel's voice saying, "Don't cry. God has promised your son a great future." Suddenly a spring of pure water gushed up from the ground.

As she brought the cool water to Ishmael's lips, Hagar was filled with gratitude, for she knew that God's mercy had saved her boy.

*...and she went down to the well,
and filled her pitcher, and came up.*
GENESIS 24:16

REBECCA AT THE WELL

The hot desert winds were blowing as Rebecca went down to the well. In the dusk she was just able to make out the forms of an old man and his camels. "A little water from your pitcher, please," he said as she came closer. "I am so thirsty." Though startled by his request and weary from her day's work, Rebecca gave him a drink, saying, "Your camels must be thirsty, too; let me water them."

The man reached into his pack and took out a golden earring and two golden bracelets, and he gave them to Rebecca. Then he asked the names of her parents. When she answered, he bowed his head and gave thanks to God, for he realized that her family was related to that of his master, Abraham. Later he told Rebecca's parents that he had been sent to find a bride for Isaac, Abraham's son. He asked that Rebecca, who had given him the water, be that bride.

And Laban had two daughters:
the name of the elder was Leah,
and the name of the younger was Rachel.
GENESIS 29:16

TWO SISTERS

Jacob loved his cousin Rachel and promised her father, Laban, that he would work seven years for her hand in marriage. Laban consented, and when the seven years had passed, he prepared a wedding feast. But Laban tricked Jacob and sent his older daughter, Leah, into the wedding tent instead of Rachel. In the morning Jacob saw what Laban had done. When he asked why, Laban said that in his country the younger sister could not marry before the older. So Jacob worked another seven years to win Rachel.

Leah was jealous of Rachel; at night she turned her face to her pillow and wept. God pitied her and allowed her to bear Jacob six sons and a daughter. Now Rachel felt envy, for she was childless. She said to Jacob, "Give me children, or else I die." Once again God felt pity, and finally Rachel, too, had sons: Joseph and Benjamin.

Jacob had twelve sons in all. Later God changed Jacob's name to Israel, and his sons became the ancestors of the twelve tribes of Israel.

*And when she could not longer hide him, she took
for him an ark of bulrushes, and daubed it with slime
and with pitch, and put the child therein;
and she laid it in the flags by the river's brink.*
EXODUS 2:3

YOKHEVED SAVES HER SON

Yokheved was desperate to protect her infant son, for Pharaoh had decreed that all Hebrew boys born in Egypt were to be killed. At first she managed to hide the baby, but after three months she dared keep him no longer. Working swiftly and secretly, Yokheved wove him a cradle of bulrushes and set it floating on the river Nile.

When Pharaoh's daughter went to the river to bathe, she saw the cradle and sent her maid to fetch it. The baby cried when she lifted him up, and Pharaoh's daughter felt pity for the child. She knew that she had found a Hebrew baby but vowed to bring him up as her own. She called him Moses, and he was raised as a prince in Egypt.

...and all the women went out after her with timbrels and with dances.

EXODUS 15:20

MIRIAM DANCES

The children of Israel had been enslaved in Egypt for many generations. But Moses, directed by God, led thousands of his people out of Egypt to freedom. The prophet Miriam, Moses' sister, went with him. When they reached the Red Sea, Moses stretched out his hands over the water, and God caused the waves to part, leaving dry land on which they could walk. But the Egyptians who came charging after them were engulfed in swirling waters.

When Miriam saw that her people had been saved from their enemies and were free at last, she could not contain her happiness. She picked up a tambourine and began a wild, exultant dance.

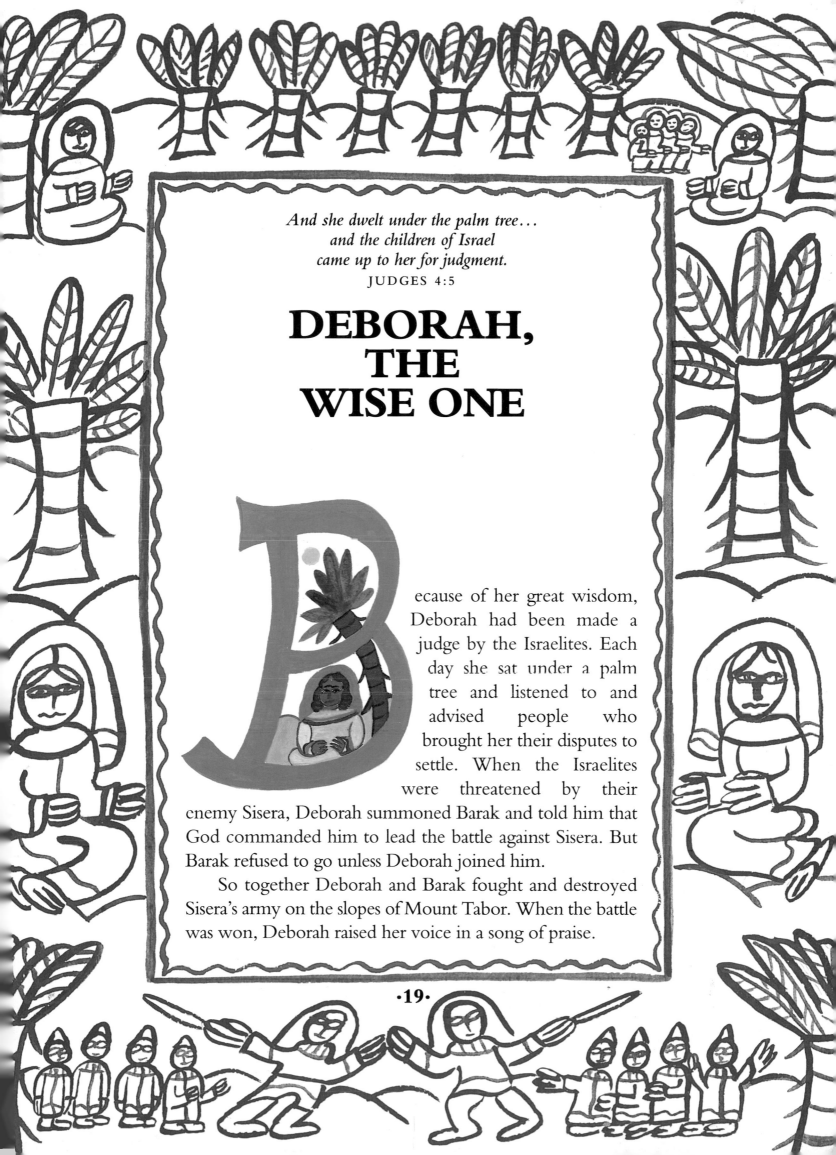

*And she dwelt under the palm tree...
and the children of Israel
came up to her for judgment.*
JUDGES 4:5

DEBORAH, THE WISE ONE

Because of her great wisdom, Deborah had been made a judge by the Israelites. Each day she sat under a palm tree and listened to and advised people who brought her their disputes to settle. When the Israelites were threatened by their enemy Sisera, Deborah summoned Barak and told him that God commanded him to lead the battle against Sisera. But Barak refused to go unless Deborah joined him.

So together Deborah and Barak fought and destroyed Sisera's army on the slopes of Mount Tabor. When the battle was won, Deborah raised her voice in a song of praise.

·19·

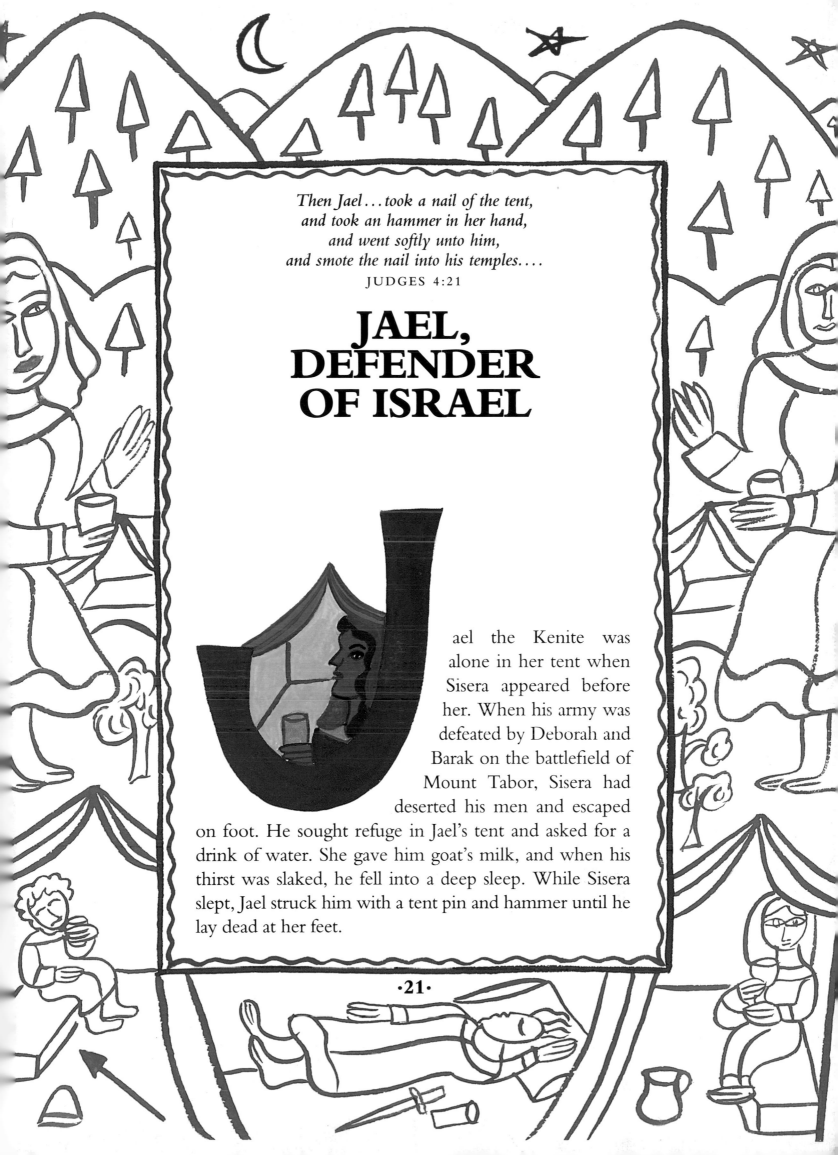

Then Jael...took a nail of the tent,
and took an hammer in her hand,
and went softly unto him,
and smote the nail into his temples....
JUDGES 4:21

JAEL, DEFENDER OF ISRAEL

ael the Kenite was alone in her tent when Sisera appeared before her. When his army was defeated by Deborah and Barak on the battlefield of Mount Tabor, Sisera had deserted his men and escaped on foot. He sought refuge in Jael's tent and asked for a drink of water. She gave him goat's milk, and when his thirst was slaked, he fell into a deep sleep. While Sisera slept, Jael struck him with a tent pin and hammer until he lay dead at her feet.

*...thy people shall be my people,
and thy God my God.*
RUTH 1:16

RUTH IN ALIEN CORN

Ruth the Moabite didn't know what to do. After the death of Ruth's husband, her mother-in-law, Naomi, urged her to remain in Moab with her own people while she herself returned to Judah. But how could Ruth let an old woman make such a trip alone? She realized she loved Naomi too much to part from her, so Ruth left the land of her childhood for an unknown life in a strange country.

The journey was long, but finally Naomi and Ruth reached Judah, land of Naomi's birth and home of her cousin Boaz. Because Naomi knew a widow's loneliness all too well, she arranged Ruth's marriage to Boaz. And when Ruth bore Boaz a child, Naomi rejoiced as if he had been her own grandson.

*...as long as he liveth
he shall be lent to the Lord.*
I SAMUEL 1:28

HANNAH'S GIFT

n her way to the temple Hannah looked down into the face of her young son, Samuel. She remembered how unhappy she had been and how she had prayed to God for a child. She had prayed ceaselessly day and night, her lips mouthing the words without uttering a sound. Hannah had made a vow that if she were blessed with a boy, she would give him to God. Now Hannah was fulfilling her sacred promise by bringing Samuel to the temple at Shiloh, where he would be raised as a priest.

*...David sent us unto thee,
to take thee to him to wife.*
I SAMUEL 25:40

ABIGAIL, A WOMAN OF GOOD SENSE

A bigail learned that Nabal, her husband, had insulted the young warrior David, and now David's men were planning to attack them. Without telling Nabal, Abigail loaded her donkeys with loaves of bread, bottles of wine, corn, raisins, fig cakes, and the bodies of five sheep prepared for cooking. Then she rode down the hill with the gift-laden donkeys and presented them to David. Kneeling, Abigail begged him to pardon her husband. Touched by her words, David forgave the insult.

Later, when Nabal died, David asked Abigail to be his wife. And after the deaths of King Saul and Saul's son Jonathan in battle, David became the king of Israel.

*And when the queen of Sheba
heard of the fame of Solomon…
she came to prove him with hard questions.*
I KINGS 10:1

THE QUEEN OF SHEBA VISITS KING SOLOMON

The queen of Sheba was known far and wide for her beauty, her wisdom, and her wealth. But she had heard so many stories about the riches and wisdom of King Solomon, who ruled over Israel, that she grew curious. Was he as clever as she? As rich? She had to find out. She ordered her servants to load her camels with precious jewels, with gold, and with spices, and she set out to visit King Solomon's court. Once there, she asked the king many riddles, each one harder than the next. Solomon solved them all.

"When I first heard of your wisdom, I didn't believe it," confessed the queen of Sheba. "But now I am convinced." Then she and the king exchanged many rare and costly gifts, and satisfied with what she had seen, the queen of Sheba returned home.

·29·

And the king said again unto Esther...
What is thy petition, queen Esther?
and it shall be granted thee....
ESTHER 7:2

ESTHER, DAUGHTER OF HER PEOPLE

Beautiful Queen Esther had never told her husband, King Ahasuerus, that she was Jewish, for her kinsman Mordecai had warned her to keep it secret. But when the king's counselor Haman wanted all the Jews put to death, Mordecai asked Queen Esther to plead with the king to save the Jews.

Though Esther feared that the king would be angry if she interfered in matters of state, she put on her royal robes and prepared a magnificent banquet for him. During the banquet she begged that the lives of her people be spared. Moved by her courage and loyalty, the king granted her wish and punished the evil Haman. The Jewish feast of Purim is celebrated to commemorate Queen Esther's bravery.

AFTERWORD

As long as the Bible has existed, there have been people—
Jews and Christians alike—who have sought to understand,
explain, and enlarge upon its meanings. For while the narrative
style is often spare, it is never unyielding, and throughout the text
there are grace-filled moments that resonate with a wealth of
personal feelings and understandable human emotion. Many of
these moments—Ruth's refusal to leave Naomi, Hagar's wish to
be spared the sight of her child's death—concern women.

In the Old Testament a patriarchal vision is ever-present, and
most women are noted because of their relationships—mother,
daughter, wife, concubine—to men who played key roles in the
early history of the Jews. Yet there is something haunting about
these women; their words and deeds transcend the limitations of
their historical context.

For this book we chose to retell and illustrate episodes in the
lives of fourteen women in order to show the more personal,
human aspects of the powerful biblical narratives and make them
accessible and meaningful to even the youngest readers.

These ancient stories act not only as windows, allowing us a
glimpse into lives gone by, but also as mirrors that reflect deep
truths about our own.

—*Yona Zeldis McDonough*
—*Malcah Zeldis*